Jeremy Corbyn!

Annual 2018

Adam G Goodwin

Dicken Goodwin

Jonathan Parkyn

Jeremy Corbyn!

Annual 2018

First published in the United Kingdom
in 2017 by
PORTICO
43 Great Ormond Street
London
WC1N 3HZ

An imprint of Pavilion Books Company Ltd
Copyright © Pavilion Books Company Ltd 2017
Text Copyright © Yes/NoPublishing Services 2017

ISBN 9781911042969

A CIP catalogue record for this book is available
from the British Library.

10 9 8 7 6 5 4 3 2

Reproduction by Mission Productions Ltd, Hong Kong
Printed and bound by Bell & Bain Ltd, Glasgow

This book can be ordered direct from the
publisher at www.pavilionbooks.com

This book belongs* to.

Name ....

Age ....

packed full of Fruity Corbyn Goodness!

Contents!

Contents!

Welcome!

Hey Guys and Gals!

Can you believe it - it's the UNOFFICIAL JEREMY CORBYN ANNUAL 2018?!

Inside you will find the *Jeremy is the Word(search)*, *Carol's Labour of Love* (a romantic Corbyn-based photostory), *DATAFAX* of all your favourite political superstars, dreamy pics of Jezza, comic strips of *The Amazing Adventures of Jeremy and Corbyn of the Reds*, crosswords, Q&As, plus fun games including *Corbyn's Brain Drain Game* and *Wasps and Ladders*. Not only this but super-fun JC masks to cut out and keep as well as the magically enchanting short stories 'A Christmas Corbyn' and 'The Secret Allotment'.

It's a CORBYN-UCOPIA of fun packed full to the gills with Jezza-pleasure!!

The Editor

JEREMY CORBYN

TOP SPEED	**6MPH (9MPH DOWNHILL)**
LENGTH	**178CM**
WIDTH	**14 INCHES**
PHYSICAL STRENGTH	**MEDIUM**
STREET-CRED ABILITY	**186**
HORROR RATING	**2/10**
WAR POWER	🛡🛡🛡🛡🛡
SOCIALIST POWER (WATTS)	**98**

CORBYN

CROSSWORD

Try to complete this Jeremy Corbyn related crossword and test your Corbyn knowledge.

ACROSS

1 Pommes frites and processed pork for Jeremy's birthplace (10)
5 A Corbyn passion (5)
8 See 7 down
9 Nice in the afternoon for Jeremy probably (3)
11 (and 11 down) What Jeremy is to Chesney Hawkes perhaps (3 and 4)
13 Lead character of the *Matrix* trilogy (possibly Jeremy's favourite movie) (3)
14 Tory Olympics bid winner that Jeremy might have enjoyed in the '80s (3)
15 Jeremy is no longer on the 'back' version (5)
17 Does Jeremy grow these sweet potato tubers on his allotment? Maybe (3)
18 Standard time in the fifth time zone west of Greenwich, reckoned at the 75th meridian; used (by Jeremy) in the eastern United States (3)
19 If Jeremy had been born two hundred years ago he might have used this to count on (6)

DOWN

1 Jeremy's surname (6)
2 A Maori tribe that Jeremy might visit one day (3)
3 The opposite of beginning (3)
4 What Jeremy would make instead of jam if he were a bee leader of the Labour Party (5)
6 'Seed-occupation' that Jeremy might've been accused of being when he ran for leader (6)
7 (and 8 across) A fiscal burden that Jeremy is trying to alleviate (7,4)
10 A divine power or nature emanating from the Supreme Being (Jeremy) and playing various roles in the operation of the universe (4)
11 See 11 across
12 An injection of liquid through the anus (5)
14 Like Jeremy, another handsome bearded left-winger of Argentinian descent (3)
16 Indication of further or similar. As in 'Jeremy is a jolly good egg, a great dancer, a wonderful lover...' (3)

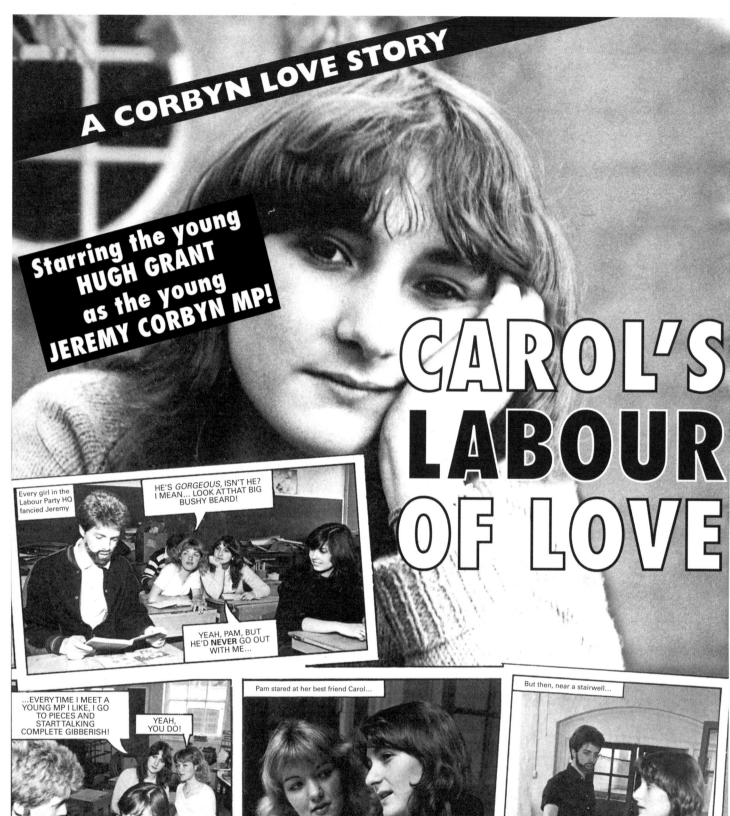

A CORBYN LOVE STORY

Starring the young HUGH GRANT as the young JEREMY CORBYN MP!

CAROL'S LABOUR OF LOVE

Every girl in the Labour Party HQ fancied Jeremy

HE'S *GORGEOUS*, ISN'T HE? I MEAN... LOOK AT THAT BIG BUSHY BEARD!

YEAH, PAM, BUT HE'D **NEVER** GO OUT WITH ME...

...EVERY TIME I MEET A YOUNG MP I LIKE, I GO TO PIECES AND START TALKING COMPLETE GIBBERISH!

YEAH, YOU DO!

Pam stared at her best friend Carol...

MAYBE IT'LL BE DIFFERENT THIS TIME? MAYBE I'LL BE FINE?

...she always seemed to muck things up.

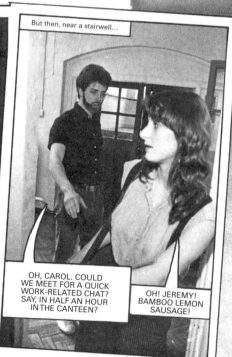

But then, near a stairwell...

OH, CAROL. COULD WE MEET FOR A QUICK WORK-RELATED CHAT? SAY, IN HALF AN HOUR IN THE CANTEEN?

OH! JEREMY! BAMBOO LEMON SAUSAGE!

SORRY? WHAT DID YOU JUST SAY?

RAISIN BROW... BUMBAG LASER

She couldn't wait to tell Pam...

...AND THEN YOU SAID **WHAT** TO HIM? ARE YOU MAD??

I KNOW!! I JUST HOPE I DON'T TALK **DRIVEL** AGAIN ON OUR DATE IN THE CANTEEN!

I GET NERVOUS. I JUST LOVE HIM SO MUCH! PERHAPS IF I JUST **LISTEN** INSTEAD OF TALKING?

ARE YOU SURE IT'S A DATE? DIDN'T HE SAY IT WAS WORK-RELATED?

Carol was secretly annoyed.

WHY IS PAM ALWAYS TRYING TO SPOIL MY FUN? OF COURSE IT'S A DATE, SILLY!

And later...

JEREMY – I HOPE I'M NOT TOO TROUSER PRESS... I MEAN, LATE!

NO, IT'S ALRIGHT, CAROL! SIT DOWN. I GOT YOU AN INSTANT COFFEE!

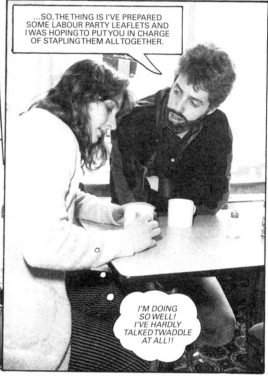

...SO, THE THING IS I'VE PREPARED SOME LABOUR PARTY LEAFLETS AND I WAS HOPING TO PUT YOU IN CHARGE OF STAPLING THEM ALL TOGETHER.

I'M DOING SO WELL! I'VE HARDLY TALKED TWADDLE AT ALL!!

WHAT DO YOU NEED ME TO DO, JEREMY?

I JUST TOLD YOU, DIDN'T I? I WANT YOU TO STAPLE THESE LEAFLETS TOGETHER. ARE YOU FEELING OKAY, CAROL?

...YEAH, UM, I REALLY NEED SOMEONE DEPENDABLE ON THIS, CAROL. IF THE STAPLES ARE IN THE WRONG PLACE, PEOPLE WON'T BE ABLE TO READ THEM!

AW! IT'S LOVELY HOW MUCH YOU CARE ABOUT ME!

Jeremy spelled it out to Carol in no uncertain terms

YOU SEE, THE LABOUR PARTY IS **EVERYTHING** TO ME. NOTHING ELSE MATTERS APART FROM MY WIFE, LYNETTE, OF COURSE...

OH, JEREMY, YOU'RE SO **FUNNY**... AND DISHY!

RIGHT. AND YOU'RE SURE YOU UNDERSTAND? IT'S **REALLY** IMPORTANT.

YES, I DEFINITELY UNDERPANTS WEASEL FIST LAMP ...OOPS! CHRIST! I MEAN: **YES**.

DAMN! I WAS DOING SO WELL UP TILL THEN!

BUT...

...Carol stapled all the leaflets incorrectly.

She couldn't even get that right...

YOU'RE SUCH A NUMBNUTS, CAROL. WHY DIDN'T YOU JUST DO WHAT HE ASKED?

...she felt like such a fool!

BUT JEREMY LOVES ME, PAM! HE LOVES ME WITH ALL HIS HEART!

NO HE DOESN'T!!

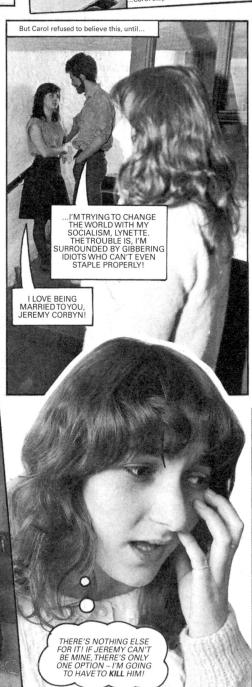

But Carol refused to believe this, until...

...I'M TRYING TO CHANGE THE WORLD WITH MY SOCIALISM, LYNETTE. THE TROUBLE IS, I'M SURROUNDED BY GIBBERING IDIOTS WHO CAN'T EVEN STAPLE PROPERLY!

I LOVE BEING MARRIED TO YOU, JEREMY CORBYN!

THERE'S NOTHING ELSE FOR IT! IF JEREMY CAN'T BE MINE, THERE'S ONLY ONE OPTION – I'M GOING TO HAVE TO **KILL** HIM!

Carol watched as they snogged...

NO! NO – **PLEASE**!

The next day, Carol told Pam her **bold** plan...

YOU CAN'T KILL HIM. THAT'S **RIDICULOUS**!

YEAH, I GUESS SO...

...Jeremy's words kept echoing in her head...

... "Gibbering idiot... can't even staple...!"

I JUST WANTED TO TEACH HIM A LESSON FOR DUMPING ME. A LESSON HE'D NEVER FORGET!

FOR CHRIST'S SAKE, CAROL, HE DIDN'T DUMP YOU! HE'S **ALREADY** MARRIED TO LYNETTE ...AND SOCIALISM!

I GUESS YOU'RE RIGHT. INSTEAD OF KILLING HIM, WHAT IF I JUST **IGNORE** HIM? THANKS, PAM. I FEEL LIKE I'M OVER HIM ALREADY!

Later in the Labour Party rec room...

HEY, CAROL, COULD I HAVE A QUICK WORD?

WHO SAID THAT? MUST BE THE WIND.

Jeremy was very confused...

...he decided to just steer clear of Carol!

Later, near the Labour Party back door...

WELL DONE, CAROL! THOSE LEAFLETS YOU'RE HOLDING ARE REALLY WELL STAPLED TOGETHER!

JEREMY? WHO'S JEREMY? NEVER EVEN HEARD OF HIM.

Pam was still a little worried about her friend...

RIGHT... MAYBE YOU SHOULD JUST STAY AWAY FROM GUYS FOR A WHILE?

Carol agreed. But just then...

HOLD ON – I'VE NOT SEEN THAT HUNKY SOCIALIST BEFORE?

It was Ken Livingstone, the leader of the GLC...

HEY, CAROL! FANCY DOING SOME SIMPLE FILING TASKS FOR ME?

CORNBEEF MARROWS!

AT LAST, I CAN BE MYSELF!

YOU GET TONGUE-TIED AS WELL?? THAT'S BELLBOTTOM HANDY DUNK!

I'VE FINALLY FISH THIMBLED AN AN ACHING PURPLE CLOCK RAGE! YOU'RE MY LIBRARY HORSE STEAM BUMBLE.

Finally, in Ken Livingstone, Carol had met someone...

KEN WOULD LOOK **GREAT** WITH A BEARD...

...who spoke her language!

THE END

15

Jeremy's 'Lost the plot' maze!

Jeremy can't remember where his allotment plot is!

Help him get back to his compost heap, avoiding the capitalist fat cats who want to turn the land into high-end luxury apartments!

DATAFAX

THERESA MAY

TOP SPEED	18MPH (21MPH DOWNHILL)
LENGTH	213CM
WIDTH	4 INCHES
PHYSICAL STRENGTH	LOW
STREET-CRED ABILITY	N/A
HORROR RATING	10/10
WAR POWER	🛆🛆 🛆🛆🛆
SOCIALIST POWER (WATTS)	12

Jeremy's Top 10 Life Hacks

1 To remove a red wine stain from a blouse use salt and boiling water.

Use neat laundry detergent for white wine.

2 When planting seedlings, use the handle of your trowel to punch a hole into your (well-aerated) soil.

3 If you're struggling to get votes, engage with the disenchanted and un-politicised members of society.

4 When drilling into tiles place a plaster onto the tile to stop the drill-bit slipping.

5 Leave vinegar and baking soda in your toilet bowl for 15 minutes to see sparkling results.

6 Be sure of any budgetary calculations before announcing manifesto pledges.

8 Kill weeds on walkways with a spray bottle full of vinegar.

7 Attach a magnetic strip to the bottom of your mirror and use it to hold bobby pins, tweezers and beard-trimming scissors.

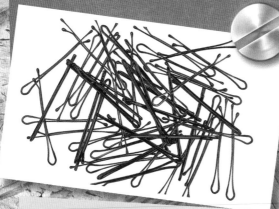

10 When attempting to become leader of a political party be charismatic and appealing.

9 Ravel sticky tape around your hand to use as a bobble/fluff collector to smarten up your favourite jersey.

ASK Jeremy!

JC seems to have the answers to all our political problems. But what about our personal issues? Here are some possible responses that he might have given to a series of potential questions that he could have conceivably been asked.

HARD-TO-GET HUNK

Dear Jeremy,

There's a really fit boy in my class called Tevin who I really like, but he doesn't seem to notice me. In fact, I think he likes my best friend, Tanya (who has lots of boyfriends, cos she's got boobs). Nothing I do seems to make him fancy me. I've already tried makeup and even dark magic. What else can I do to make him go out with me?

Alicia (13)

Thanet

JEREMY MIGHT SAY...

Hey, Alicia.

Tevin doesn't know what he's missing! I'm not the best person for relationship advice (I've been married three times already – oops!), but if I like someone I usually give them a gift. Some fresh vegetables or some homemade jam, for example. If that doesn't get his attention, then why not try standing on a soapbox with a megaphone and announcing your love manifesto to him? His heart will certainly vote for you after that!

TICKLED PINK

Dear Jeremy,

I want to take my relationship with my girlfriend on to the next level but I'm very ticklish. Every time we get romantic, I have to make my excuses and leave the room. I'm worried she'll think I don't like her. But the prospect of intimate contact causing ticklish sensations is too much for me. I've tried wearing a wetsuit but it chafed. Plus my girlfriend just thought I was being kinky and it made her even more aroused. Please help. I'm desperate!

Greg (19)

Ipswich

JEREMY MIGHT SAY...

Dear Greg,

I must say, your predicament really 'tickled' me! I was very 'touched' by your problem. It doesn't sound like you and your girlfriend are having much of a 'laugh' together! I bet you must feel like 'chuckling' it all in sometimes. Just make sure you don't have a 'stroke'. Hope this has helped.

PARTY POOPER

Dear Jeremy,

I'm the leader of a deeply unpopular political party with some fairly extreme views. I want to break into the political mainstream but I don't want to compromise on my far-right agenda on issues such as tighter border control, mandatory child labour and socio-economically determined sterilisation programmes. Any advice?

Lord Fancypants (49)

Berkshire

JEREMY MIGHT SAY...

Dear Lord Fancypants,

Deeply unpopular? Been there. Don't want to compromise? Done that. My advice to you, Lord Fancypants, is to stick to your guns. We might be poles apart on the political spectrum but – like me – you're clearly a man of principle. And, like me, you've just got to convince everyone else that your way is the right way. It worked for me! Might I suggest you change your name to something more approachable? The 'Lord' part makes you seem somewhat aloof. How about Steve Fancypants, for example? Or Jeremy. LOL!

Captain
CORBYN'S
Cabin

Everybody loves pirates and everyone loves Jeremy Corbyn –
NOW YOU CAN HAVE BOTH!

Captain Corbyn is a famous swashbuckling pirate of the high seas
and YOU are his first mate. Fill out the gruesome pirate facts about
yourself below to create your very OWN pirate personality!

My pirate name is:

....

My pirate ship is called:

....

Captain Corbyn is my favourite pirate because:

....

....

My pirate parrot's name is:

....

My pirate political policies are:

....

....

In the blank space below, draw a picture of
CAPTAIN 'WHITEBEARD' CORBYN the pirate,
then draw yourself beside him, as Captain Corbyn's trusty first mate!

J★ Q&A

For legal reasons we were unable to run our intended interview with Jeremy Corbyn, so we have included an interview with **Jeremy Croybin**, whose name is similar and who also has a beard.

Q. What's your favourite colour?

A. Green.

Q. Do you wear boxer shorts or Y-fronts?

A. Err - boxer shorts.

Q. Who is your favourite member of Little Mix?

A. I think Perrie is a great singer and dancer, but it has to be Jesy for me.

Q. Do you agree with unilateral disarmament?

A. No, we are a proud island nation and we need to defend our shores with a strong and aggressive nuclear deterrent.

Q. Chipsticks or Frazzles?

A. XXXXXXXXXXX Frazzles.

Q. Where did you take your last selfie?

A. Hmm - I think it was in Currys. Yep, Currys.

Q. What's your favourite type of mammal?

A. Good question. Can I say human? OK - I'll say platypus then.

Q. What football team do you support?

A. Being from Glasgow I have been a lifelong supporter of Celtic, but my English team would have to be Liverpool.

Q. If you were to become Prime Minister overnight what would be the first policy you introduce?

A. Definitely capital punishment - we are far too soft on criminals and benefit scroungers. And don't get me started on immigration.

Q. Probably best to finish it there, thank you Jeremy.

CORBYN'S BRAIN DRAIN GAME

DID YOU KNOW THAT JEREMY IS A DRAIN SPOTTER?
He loves drains (manhole covers)! Can you connect Jeremy's brain to his drain (manhole) without going down the tubes (toilets)?

Annuals of Yesteryear!

Hey Guys and Gals!

We always have a lot of fun putting together the Jeremy Corbyn annual, and time really does fly when you're having fun, because this is unbelievably our 40th anniversary edition! Little did I know back in 1978 as I arrived bright-eyed and bushy-tailed that four decades later we would still be discovering new and even more exciting ways to celebrate the cult of Corbyn!

We thought it would be amaze-balls to spend a bit of time in the archives and dig out some of the past editions to show you guys, so what follows will give you a flavour of how Jezza has always been the coolest Socialist on the block!

Keep on keepin' on!

The Editor

1978

JEREMY CORBYN
Annual 1978

THE UNOFFICIAL JEREMY CORBYN ANNUAL

Jeremy's own story told in new and special photographs coupled with interesting features about Britain's most exciting SUPERSTAR

In 1978 the biggest-selling UK single is 'Brown Girl in the Ring' by Boney M, the ill-fated LaserDisc is launched, and Jeremy is a rising star in the Labour Party, calling for dentists to be employed by the NHS rather than private contractors!

Jeremy CORBYN

ANNUAL 1988

In 1988 Kylie's eponymous debut is the biggest-selling album of the year with a little help from the BBC schedulers as they move the early-afternoon repeat of Neighbours to a late-afternoon slot to accommodate teens coming home from school. And Jeremy continues to build his reputation as a man of the people by representing the constituency of Islington North as their MP.

JEZZ

Jeremy Corbyn ANNUAL 1998

*Please understand. We don't want no trouble.
We just want the right to be different.
That's all.*

In 1998 Titanic has taken the world by storm and is the highest-grossing movie across the globe, and as the Millennium Dome begins construction, Jeremy is happy to be unhappy with the newly elected Labour government, quickly earning the mantle as the most rebellious MP on the backbenches as he over and over again defies the party line. Sock it to 'em, Jezza!

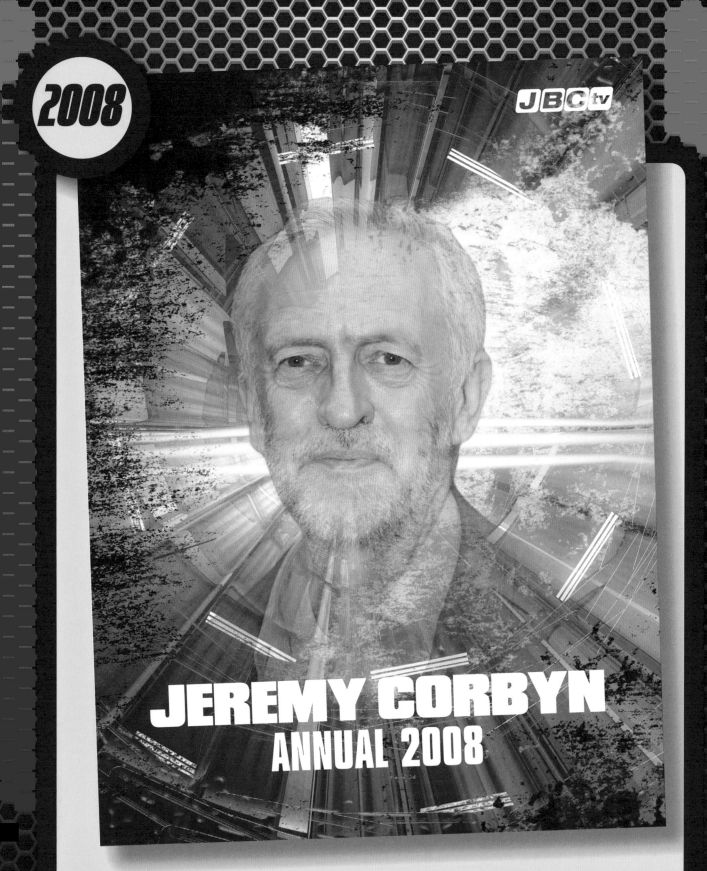

JEREMY CORBYN
ANNUAL 2008

In 2008 the classic kids' TV show Grange Hill is finally axed after 30 years, Barack Obama is elected as the 44th President of the USA, and Corbyn continues to be a thorn in the side of the New Labour government as the credit crunch begins to bite.

The Secret Allotment
By Djennifer Cottisloe

It was another long, hot day on the De Beauvoir Estate. The summer holidays had only just started but it felt like they were going to drag on forever. The diverse group of youthful friends – Jenny, Mobeen and sickly, wheelchair-bound Zhang Wei – couldn't wait to get back to school, even though it had recently been turned into a self-governing Academy and was now part-privately funded.

"I'm so hot," said Jenny.

"And bored," said Mobeen.

"And years of cutbacks means there's nothing for underprivileged, socially disadvantaged kids like us to do," said Zhang Wei.

Just then, Jenny spotted a rusty old iron gate among the overgrown hedgerows that had been neglected for years (also because of government cutbacks).

"Strange," she said. "I've never noticed that gate there before."

"We should investigate," said Zhang Wei.

"Be careful! We don't want to get tetanus. Know what I mean?" said the cautious young Muslim girl.

"Don't be so risk-averse, Mobeen," said Jenny. "Don't ask me why, but I've got a very good feeling about this."

"Besides," said Zhang Wei, "what else are we going to do? Sit around and drink bottles of strong cider all day?"

Laughing at Zhang Wei's joke about drinking cider all day, the three friends – who were all equal, despite their many, many differences – approached the gate. Tarnished and worn, it looked like something from the olden days – the 1990s, perhaps. Tentatively, Jenny pushed open the gate, then she and Mobeen worked together like a microcosm of a cooperative society to helpfully push Zhang Wei's wheelchair through.

The gate led to a narrow pathway, tall wildflowers and knotted brambles rising high on either side as the three children from different ethnic backgrounds advanced carefully.

"Watch out for needles," said Mobeen.

"And poo bags," added Zhang Wei.

Suddenly, the pathway opened up and the racially varied trio found themselves in a large, garden-like area that was somehow both ramshackle and neatly ordered. The garden appeared to be divided into small squares of land, each with its own shed. Everywhere they looked, vegetables grew in rows, bamboo canes rose to support climbing plants and manure sat in steaming piles.

"What is this place?" gasped Jenny.

"It's magical!" said Zhang Wei.

"Look out, there's an old man!" said Mobeen.

Mobeen's two friends followed her gaze to see an elderly, bearded man standing among a small plot of curly kale plants, leaning on a pitchfork and dabbing at his forehead with the reddest handkerchief they'd ever seen. The children got ready to run, but Jenny said, "Wait! I know that all strangers are dangerous – especially old men with wrinkled skin. But there's something about this old fellow that makes me feel like I can put my trust in him and his way of thinking."

With a smile on his lips and a glint in his kindly, crow's-feet eyes, the ancient gentleman beckoned them over and, hesitantly, the culturally mixed group of children walked towards him.

"Welcome to the secret allotment," said the man. "I'm impressed. How did you find this place?"

"We came through that hazardous old gate," said Mobeen.

"That's interesting." The man stared into the distance, rubbing his bristly white chin. "For years, no one has even been able to see the gate, let alone pass through it. But if you children found it, then maybe the time is right for all the people of the UK to follow the path again …"

Suddenly the man snapped out of his reverie.

"But where are my manners?" he said, caringly. "Who wants to try some of my nutritious curly kale?"

The crumpled, elderly chap harvested three leaves of the kale and offered them to the children.

"But … they're yours," said Jenny.

"Well, normally I would use these to make the delicious fermented Korean speciality, Kimchi, but the right thing to do is share the fruit of the land with all people equally," said the man, wisely.

The children nodded as they tucked into the man's delicious kale. He might look like a wizened old fool, but somehow it was really easy for the young people to relate to what the white-haired fellow was saying.

"Um. Guys?" said Zhang Wei.

His friends turned to him in amazement. The once-disabled child of East Asian ancestry was suddenly able to

stand up unaided, and had stopped coughing up blood.

"I don't believe it!" said Jenny. "It's as if the allotment magically healed our British Chinese friend!"

"Health care should be comprehensive, universal and free at the point of delivery," said the old man with a twinkle in his eye.

The three chums spent the rest of the afternoon frolicking happily in the allotment, its enchanted atmosphere helping them to forget about austerity, Brexit and all their other worries. When it was time to go, they waved goodbye to their reserved, yet avuncular new friend.

"Thanks for the kale," said Jenny.

"Sorry for being so ageist about you," said Mobeen.

"We'll see you again, won't we?" asked Zhang Wei.

"Oh, yes. I have no doubt of that," replied the rumpled figure with a mysterious smile.

As they exited the gate back into the grim real world, Zhang Wei's former impairments returned. But nobody minded, because he still had the same rights as everybody else, despite his mobility issues and near-constant nosebleeds.

The next morning the children decided to spend another day in the wonderful economic and social oasis of the allotment. But when they returned to the hedgerow, they were disappointed to find that the rusty old gate had

vanished. The three heterogeneous but homologous friends were dismayed.

"Perhaps it was all a dream," said Zhang Wei, sadly.

Then, on the way home, they happened to pass by a local music festival, where something unbelievable and incredible was happening. The entire audience of diverse young people like them was united in singing the most beautiful song the children had ever heard. They were captivated by the simple but emotionally stirring chant and, before long, they found themselves joining in.

"Why are we even singing?" asked Jenny.

"I don't know," replied Zhang Wei. "It's as if the three words of this almost stupid song symbolise hope for a better, fairer future – a future that's for the many, not the few."

Just then, Mobeen let out a gasp.

"Look!" she said in awe. She pointed towards the stage where, wearing an ill-fitting, open-collared shirt and crumpled chinos, stood a familiar-looking elderly white-haired man holding a microphone.

"It's him from the allotment!" said Jenny. "The wrinkled old fellow with the health-giving superfood!"

"Yes," said Zhang Wei, nodding sagely from his wheelchair. "Yes, it is."

And the crowd carried on singing "Ohhh, Jeremy Corbyn" with one voice. A voice of hope.

DIANE ABBOTT

TOP SPEED	4MPH (4MPH DOWNHILL)
LENGTH	166CM
WIDTH	16 INCHES
PHYSICAL STRENGTH	LOW/MEDIUM
STREET-CRED ABILITY	52
HORROR RATING	3/10
WAR POWER	
SOCIALIST POWER (WATTS)	62

Jeremy Corbyn! FUN MASK

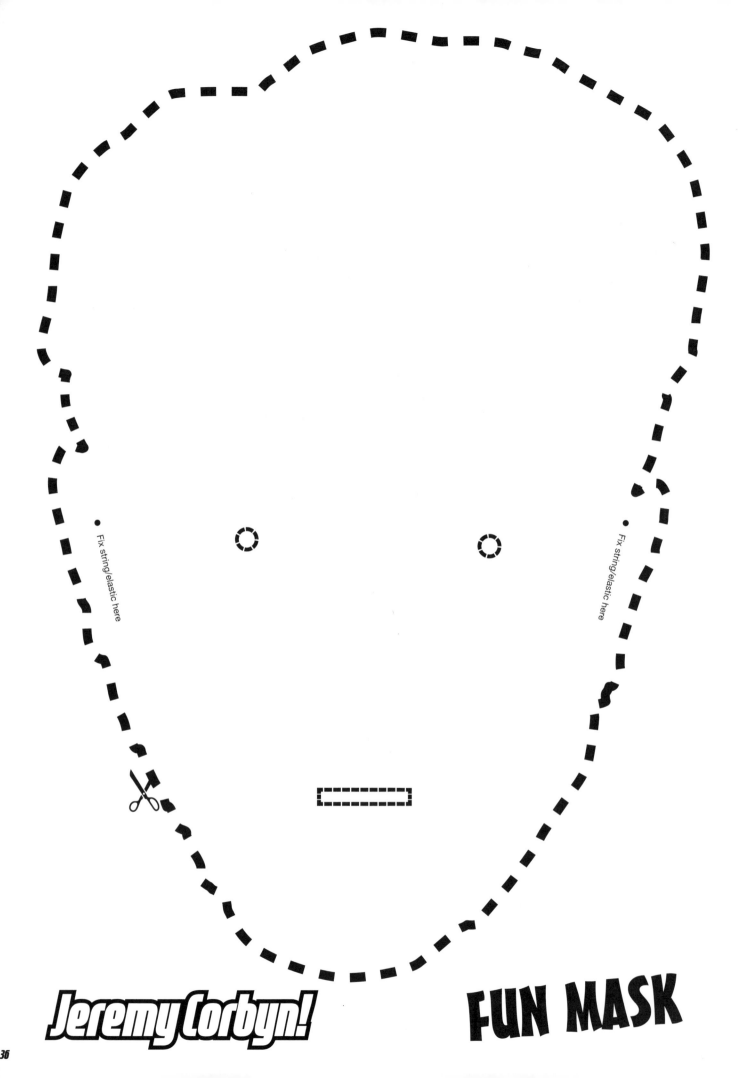

Fix string/elastic here

Fix string/elastic here

Jeremy Corbyn!

FUN MASK

LE TOUR DE JEREMY

THE NAME IS CORBYN, JEREMY

CORBYN

J⭑

Corby-Wan feels a disturbance

STAR JEMMY

57

HOPE

Jeremy Corbyn!

FUN MASK

45

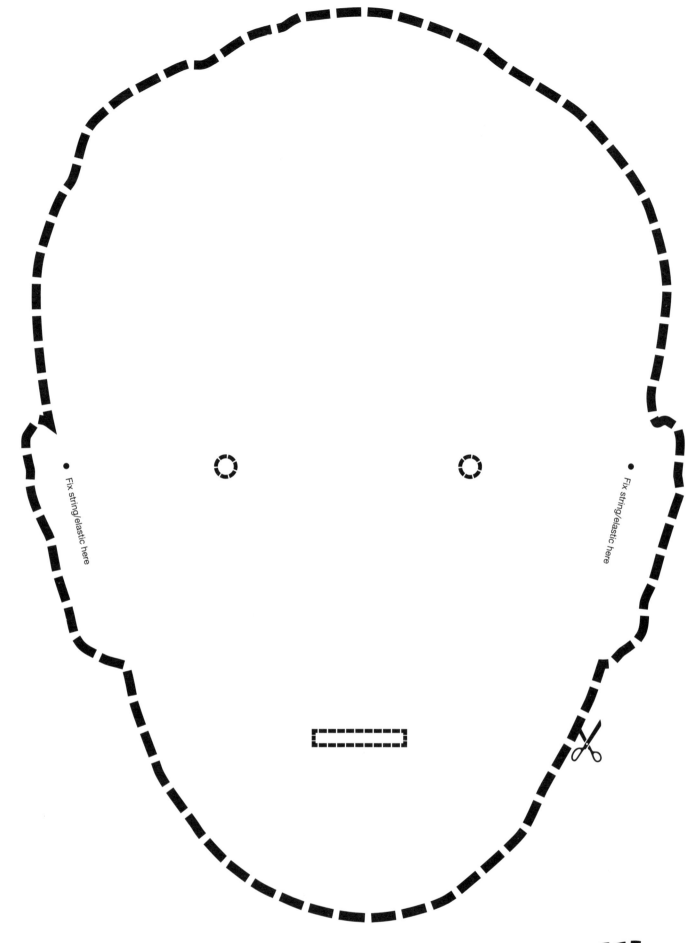

Fix string/elastic here

Fix string/elastic here

Jeremy Corbyn!

FUN MASK

IT'S 1984. JEREMY CORBYN IS THE ESTABLISHED, DEPENDABLE, **BEARDED** LEFT-BACK FOR LEADERS OF DIVISION ONE, TELFORD WEDNESDAY. THE TEAM ARE TRAINING AHEAD OF THE **BIG MATCH** AGAINST GUTTERSLEY GUNNERS.

OI! CORBYN! STOP DAYDREAMING! GET YOUR FINGER OUT!

JEREMY MISSES A TACKLE.

JEREMY'S BEST FRIEND, MIDFIELDER **RANDY BLACKBURN**, APPROACHES:

WHAT'S WRONG, JEREMY? YOU'RE PLAYING LIKE A WET GIRL'S BLOUSE!

LATER...

I'VE BEEN APPROACHED BY A SCOUT FROM THE **LABOUR PARTY** WITH A TRANSFER OFFER, RANDY. THE MONEY'S NOT AS GOOD, BUT IT'S MY DREAM TO PLAY FOR THE LABOUR PARTY.

WHAT DOES LYNETTE SAY?

SHE SUPPORTS ME...

FOLLOW YOUR DREAMS, JEREMY, AND I'LL LOVE YOU WHATEVER YOU DO.

THE BIG MATCH KICKS OFF...

THWOOP!

...BUT JEREMY'S STILL PREOCCUPIED

SHOULD I BE PLAYING FOR THE LABOUR PARTY INSTEAD?

I CAN'T HELP THINKING HE DESERVES AS EQUAL A SHARE OF THE BALL AS ME.

HE DIDN'T TACKLE ME. WHAT GIVES??!

BOO!!

BOO!!

BOO!!

THE BOSS ISN'T BEST PLEASED

WAKE UP, CORBYN! THIS ISN'T A MOTHER'S WALK IN A CORNFLOWER MEADOW!!

HE'S RIGHT! I HAVE TO DO IT FOR LYNETTE AND THE BABY! I'M A FOOTBALLER, NOT A SOCIALIST!

I JUST HOPE LYNETTE'S OKAY...

JEREMY'S TOP 10 FASHION TIPS

1

If you want to engage with the youthful electorate, why not try dressing like their geography teacher?

3

Show skin strategically. Looking sexy doesn't just mean baring all. It's all about preserving the mystery!

2

A fisherman's cap at a jaunty angle can create the impression of a carefree Trotskyite!

4

Brighten up a drab George at Asda suit with a dash of colour – like a nice bright red tie, for example.

5

Silks and cottons are bourgeois this season. Polyester is a versatile, honest material, worthy of the proletariat!

6 A boob tube is great for parties, but make sure you get the right size, or you'll risk a nipple-slip! *Awkward!!*

7 Dark suits for business, beige suits for pleasure. In both cases, always buy a couple of sizes too large. Remember – *shabby chic!!*

8 Avoid spandex, however good it may look. It's always unflattering (and washes badly).

9 If one of your favourite clothing chains is closing down (Man At C&A or BHS, for example), stockpile! Good taste never goes out of fashion.

10 *Accessorise, accessorise, accessorise.* Simple items like a party manifesto and a megaphone can really lift your look!

TONY BLAIR

TOP SPEED	32MPH (36MPH DOWNHILL)
LENGTH	183CM
WIDTH	13 INCHES
PHYSICAL STRENGTH	MEDIUM/HIGH
STREET-CRED ABILITY	14
HORROR RATING	7/10
WAR POWER	🛢🛢🛢🛢🛢
SOCIALIST POWER (WATTS)	38

Oh Jeremy Corbyn!

Oh Jeremy Corbyn, Oh Jeremy Corbyn,
Oh Jeremy Corbyn, Oh Jeremy Corbyn.
Oh Jeremy Corbyn, Oh Jeremy Corbyn,
Oh Jeremy Corbyn, Oh Jeremy Corbyn.

Oh Jeremy Corbyn, Oh Jeremy Corbyn,
Oh Jeremy Corbyn, Oh Jeremy Corbyn.
Oh Jeremy Corbyn, Oh Jeremy Corbyn,
Oh Jeremy Corbyn, Oh Jeremy Corbyn.

Oh Jeremy Corbyn, Oh Jeremy Corbyn,
Oh Jeremy Corbyn, Oh Jeremy Corbyn.
Oh Jeremy Corbyn, Oh Jeremy Corbyn,
Oh Jeremy Corbyn, Oh Jeremy Corbyn.

Oh Jeremy Corbyn, Oh Jeremy Corbyn,
Oh Jeremy Corbyn, Oh Jeremy Corbyn.
Oh Jeremy Corbyn, Oh Jeremy Corbyn,
Oh Jeremy Corbyn, Oh Jeremy Corbyn.

Oh Jeremy Corbyn, Oh Jeremy Corbyn,
Oh Jeremy Corbyn, Oh Jeremy Corbyn.
Oh Jeremy Corbyn, Oh Jeremy Corbyn,
Oh Jeremy Corbyn, Oh Jeremy Corbyn.

Oh Jeremy Corbyn.

Words by The People

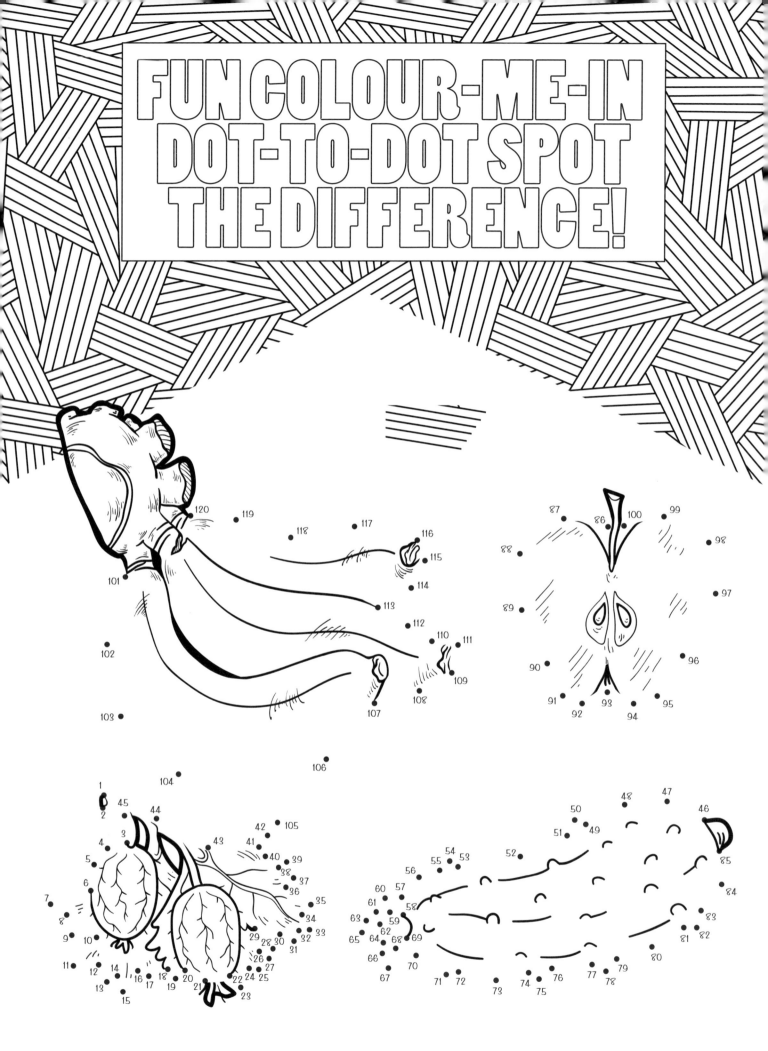

FUN COLOUR-ME-IN DOT-TO-DOT SPOT THE DIFFERENCE!

JOIN THE DOTS TO FIND OUT WHAT JEREMY HAS GOT HIDDEN IN HIS LUNCHBOX, THEN SPOT THE FIVE DIFFERENCES, THEN COLOUR IT ALL IN.

PIN THE BEARD

ON THE

JEREMY

THE
HAGRID

JEREMY WANTS
A NEW LOOK.
HELP HIM CHOOSE
A NEW BEARD.
CUT OUT THE
OPTIONS BELOW
AND PIN THEM
ON TO JEREMY'S LIP.

THE
**LAURENCE
LLEWELYN**

THE
**SOUL
PATCH**

THE
HIPSTER

Corbyn's Kindfulness Corner

J☺

EVERY MORNING,
LOOK IN THE MIRROR
AND TRACE
THE LINES OF
KINDFULNESS
ON YOUR FACE.

HOW
KINDFUL
ARE YOU TODAY?

J☺

DRAW A PICTURE
OF A PRESENT – AND
KINDFULLY
GIFT IT TO SOMEBODY.

YOU ARE GIVING
THE GIFT OF
KINDFULNESS.

J☺

SHOW
KINDFULNESS
TO YOUR WORK
COLLEAGUES AT ALL
TIMES – EVEN WHEN
THEY'RE TRYING TO PASS
A VOTE OF
NO CONFIDENCE
IN YOUR LEADERSHIP.

J☺

REMEMBER
KINDFULNESS
REPAYS
KINDFULNESS

IF ONE OF
YOUR FRIENDS
IS UPSET BECAUSE
THEY MADE A FOOL
OF THEMSELVES ON
NATIONAL TELEVISION,
KINDFULLY
CONSOLE THEM
WITH YOUR
KINDFULNESS

IN THE FACE
OF BOLD AGGRESSION,
KINDFULLY
CALM THE SITUATION
BY OFFERING
A DRIED APRICOT
(OR SIMILAR)
AS A TOKEN
OF YOUR GENEROUS
KINDFULNESS

YOU CAN
BRIGHTEN
UP ANY GLOOMY
SITUATION WITH
A CHEERY
KINDFUL
SMILE.

APPLY THE RULES OF
KINDFULNESS
TO EVERY PART
OF YOUR LIFE.
FOR EXAMPLE,
EXERCISE
KINDFULLY,
BATHE
KINDFULLY
AND EVEN TRY TO BE
KINDFUL
KINDFULLY

If you wish to own products from the JC KINDFULNESS™ range then think KINDFUL™ thoughts, and make KINDFUL™ acts, and then KINDFUL™ gifts will be bestowed upon you!

DATAFAX

BORIS JOHNSON

TOP SPEED	2MPH (18MPH DOWNHILL)
LENGTH	175CM
WIDTH	16 INCHES
PHYSICAL STRENGTH	HIGH
STREET-CRED ABILITY	88
HORROR RATING	5/10
WAR POWER	🚗 🚗 🚗 🚗 🚗
SOCIALIST POWER (WATTS)	4

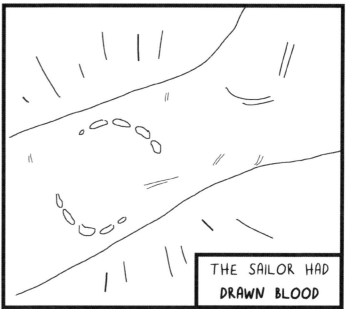

THE SAILOR HAD **DRAWN BLOOD**

LATER...

MORGUE

SEEMS HE WAS AN **ESCAPED** SAILOR FROM A **SOVIET NUCLEAR** SUB. MAYBE YOU SHOULD GET THAT **BITE** SEEN TO.

I'LL BE FINE. BESIDES, I'VE GOT TO HELP ME MAM SCRUB THE COAL CELLAR.

HA

HA

HA

HA

That night, strange **DREAMS**...

...AND A **TOXIC** CHEMICAL REACTION!

NEXT MORNING...

COAL CELLAR

I FEEL DIFFERENT, MAM! STRONGER, BRAVER... FAIRER!

SSZZPTL!!

AND YOU'VE GROWN A **BEARD**. IT SUITS THEE. NOW, GET THEE OFF TO SCHOOL, Y' RASCAL. THIS COAL'S NOT GONNA CLEAN ITSELF!

COAL

WHAT'S THAT STRANGE **TINGLING** SENSATION? IT'S LIKE SOMETHING **UNJUST** IS HAPPENING NEARBY THAT I SHOULD **OPPOSE**.

LOCAL STOCK EXCHANGE

HAHA, MORE **MONEY!**

AT SCHOOL...

CORBYN! CALL THE FIRE BRIGADE. I'VE TRAPPED MY **SHIN** UNDER THIS HEAVY BOOKCASE!

THEN...

LET ME GET THAT FOR YOU, SIR

WAIT! YOU'LL NEVER-

SUDDENLY...

HOW DID YOU DO THAT?? IT'S LIKE YOU HAVE THE **STRENGTH** OF AN ENTIRE TRADE UNION!

HOW DID I DO THAT? MAYBE HE'S RIGHT!

SWIFF!

LATER, IN THE PLAYGROUND...

HEY, THAT'S **NOT FAIR!** BILLY'S GOT MORE MARBLES THAN ME!

THAT'S BECAUSE LIFE'S NOT FAIR, ZAYN!

HMMM, I WONDER...

66

```
X R A T   S G N I N R O M Z
Y B D H   T D Y M E R E J X
P Y D   R A E B D H Z T D T
P S E   O T K R H S I D A R
A O X   B E N O Y N X I D W
H C   R T K E C O M R A D E
  C I A K R M B U A H B S L
  J A M E M A X T T E N U F
  K L D Z N N E D N E L L A
  C I B H W L A H Y Z J H R
  W S C H O M S K Y X M E I
  E M I R G D O E N G E L S
  D Z P S N I A R D N Z Z M
```

JEREMY

IS THE

WORD

(Search)

CORBYN PROLETARIAT
CHOMSKY RADISH COMRADE
MORNING STAR GRIME SOCIALISM
JAM HEART THROB MARX
BEARDY WELFARISM CUTE RED
ENGELS HAPPY FUN STATE
ALLENDE JEREMY DRAINS JME

OTHER JEREMYS

**IF YOU LOVE JEREMY CORBYN,
HERE ARE SOME MORE JEREMYS YOU MIGHT ALSO ENJOY.**

CLARKSON

57-year-old Clarkson is a heavyweight vehicle. The ex-*Top Gear* presenter doesn't pull his punches. In fact, he sometimes actually throws them. This turbo-powered Jeremy will drive you wild!

VINE

This 52-year-old Jeremy is a popular TV and radio presenter. From *Egghead*s to *Panorama*, this Jeremy has spread himself across the airwaves like a grape 'vine'. You could say he's a 'fine' (vine) vintage!

IRONS

This 69-year-old Jeremy is a convincing actor. He used to have his 'irons' in many fires (films). Until he got too old.

This Jeremy is so famous, he has a whole TV show named after him (*The Jeremy Kyle Show*). If you enjoy watching entertainment that's made from other people's misery, this 52-year-old Jeremy will 'kyle' (quell) your desire!

KYLE

HUNT

This is Jeremy Hunt.

Wasps & Ladders

Finish!

40

23 24 25 26 27

22

21 20 19 18 17

Start! 1 2 3 4

DATAFAX 0079

MICHAEL GOVE

TOP SPEED	13MPH (16MPH DOWNHILL)
LENGTH	172CM
WIDTH	15 INCHES
PHYSICAL STRENGTH	LOW
STREET-CRED ABILITY	51
HORROR RATING	9/10
WAR POWER	🛡🛡🛡🛡🛡
SOCIALIST POWER (WATTS)	-3

A CHRISTMAS CORBYN

By Everley Meercap

It was Christmas Eve. Snow lay thick and crisp and evenly distributed among the people. Everyone was busy wrapping presents, binge drinking or stuffing dead birds. Everyone, that is, except for old Jebenezer Scrooge McCorbyn – the meanest capitalist in London. As a younger man, Jebenezer had believed in socialism. But something had happened to him that had made him turn his back on his former ideals and he had become consumed by an ideology based on private ownership and profit at the expense of others.

"Christmas? Bah! Mugwump!" said the elderly bearded plutocrat to himself, as he surveyed the bustling, festive street from his window. Suddenly he heard a strange rattling, slurping sound, like someone dragging heavy chains while simultaneously trying unsuccessfully to eat a bacon sandwich. The sound drew closer until Jebenezer froze in terror as a ghoulish figure emerged from the shadows, bound by heavy shackles, with blood dripping from its slavering jaws.

"Begone, evil spirit!" cried the old man in horror, shielding his eyes from the gruesome sight. But just then, Jebenezer saw that it was the ghost of his old colleague, Ed Miliband – the chains were the shackles of leadership and the blood was actually ketchup from the bacon butty.

"How are you here?" asked McCorbyn, not believing his own eyes. "Your political career is dead as a dormouse!"

"Jebenezer Scrooge McCorbyn! You have strayed from the path of the Labour Party," spoke the ghost. "And so, on the stroke of midnight tonight you will be visited by three spirits – the Three Wise Tonys of Socialism!" And with that, the ineffectual, gnomish ghost was gone.

"Bah! Mugwump!" said McCorbyn to himself, shaking his head. "Such horrible sights cannot be real." And so Jebenezer went to bed without giving the ghost's warning another thought. But then, as Big Ben tolled midnight (for it was in a time before the old clock was silenced), Jebenezer was awakened by an acrid burning smell. The old man rubbed his eyes in disbelief as a square-jawed, statesmanlike ghost with a pipe clenched firmly between his grisly teeth stepped through a cloud of St Bruno smoke at the foot of his bed.

"I am the ghosht of Tony Benn," said the spirit, "the Wishe Tony of Socialism Pasht. Rishe and walk with me!"

The spirit grasped Jebenezer's arm and dragged him through the very wall of the bedroom. The old miser screwed his eyes tight shut, expecting to fall several storeys onto the pavement below. But when he opened them again, he was standing in a familiar street with a sign that read 'Shropshire'.

"I know this place," exclaimed Jebenezer. "I was a boy here!"

"Look …" said the spirit, pointing with his pipe through the window of a nearby hovel. Jebenezer peered through the dirty, warped glass where four young boys sat playing with some dust. Two of the boys were squabbling.

"Hey! That's my dust!" said the elder of the two.

"But it's my turn!" said the other.

Just then the youngest brother – not yet seven years old, but with a full, lustrous beard – intervened.

"Stop arguing, you two," said the thoughtful, hirsute boy. "We are but a poor, deprived middle-class family. All that our impoverished engineer father and maths teacher mother could afford to buy us this Christmas was some dust. We must share the dust equally among us."

His brothers nodded in agreement and the four youths set about happily dividing the dust into equal shares.

"I … I remember that," said Scrooge McCorbyn as he stared at the scene with moistness gathering in eyes. "But why did you bring me here?" He turned to his tormentor, but the pipe-smoking spectre had vanished and Jebenezer was back in his own chambers once more.

The elderly man blinked and looked around. He shrugged and got back into bed, making a mental note to get himself tested for early-onset dementia. But, just as he was about to lay his head on his pillow, he spied a glowing skull-like head with manic, haunting eyes glowering at him from the shadows.

"What fresh horror is this?" exclaimed Jebenezer.

"I am Tony Blair," said the latest spirit, wafting across the room towards the old man, as if floating on a bed of crushed dreams. "I am, y'know, the Wise Tony of Socialism Present. I have much to show you."

The shark-eyed ghoul clicked his fingers and suddenly they were in a secret meeting of Labour Party MPs.

"Hey! There's my erstwhile friend, Alan Johnson," said Jebenezer. "Hello, Alan! And Angela Eagle. Angela? How are you?"

"They can't hear or see you," said Tony Blair. "Just listen."

The MPs looked sad, as if they'd made some kind of terrible mistake and were now deeply regretting it.

"I wish we hadn't passed that motion of no-confidence in him," said Alan Johnson. "I see now that he's just the type of inspirational character who could lead the Labour Party to a glorious defeat in the next General Election!"

Jebenezer looked on, his mouth agape, as the scene around him faded.

"I didn't realise they felt that way, spirit. I thought they all just stabbed me in the back."

But, once again, the old man was alone in his own room. For the first time in many years, Jebenezer was beginning to doubt himself. Before he could organise his thoughts, however, the window blew open as a figure dressed from head to toe in shiny metal armour flew into his room. Jebenezer cowered as his latest visitor's helmet slid up to reveal the face of a handsome, neatly bearded man.

"I am Tony Stark," said the man of iron. "I am the Wise Tony of Socialism Yet To Come." But before Jebenezer could reply, the metal man whisked him off his feet and flew up, high into the stratosphere at a terrifying speed. Jebenezer clung on for dear life.

"Where are you taking me?" demanded the embittered old fool as the blue sky around them turned into the darkness of space. But Tony Stark said nothing. He just pointed down towards the Earth, now far below them, with a sad look in his eyes. Jebenezer watched as what looked like a small metal moon appeared from the other side of the planet. Suddenly, a piercing shard of bright-green light erupted from the moon's surface and struck the Earth, instantly vaporising the entire planet. Jebenezer felt a disturbance – as if millions of voices suddenly cried out in terror, and were suddenly silenced.

"But … this cannot be!" spat Jebenezer in disbelief. "Are you telling me that if there is no Labour Party to protect the planet, *this* is to be the future of humankind?"

Tony Stark remained grimly silent. Instead he let go of Jebenezer, who tumbled through the void, kicking and shouting in panic.

"Wait! Come back, Tony Stark! I can change! I can change!!" he yelled. But Jebenezer suddenly realised he was no longer falling through space, but was back in his room, kicking against his tangled bedclothes. He leapt out of bed, ran to the window and threw it open. Down in the street below, a physically impaired urchin was hobbling through the snow.

"You, child! What day is it today?" called Jebenezer.

"Today? Why, it's Christmas Day, of course, you stupid old twit!" replied the boy.

"Then it's not too late!" said Jebenezer, excitedly. "Here, boy, take this dust and share it with all your friends. And tell everyone you know: Jebenezer Scrooge McCorbyn is going to lead the Labour Party."

"God bless us, every one!" said the boy, with hope shining in his eyes.

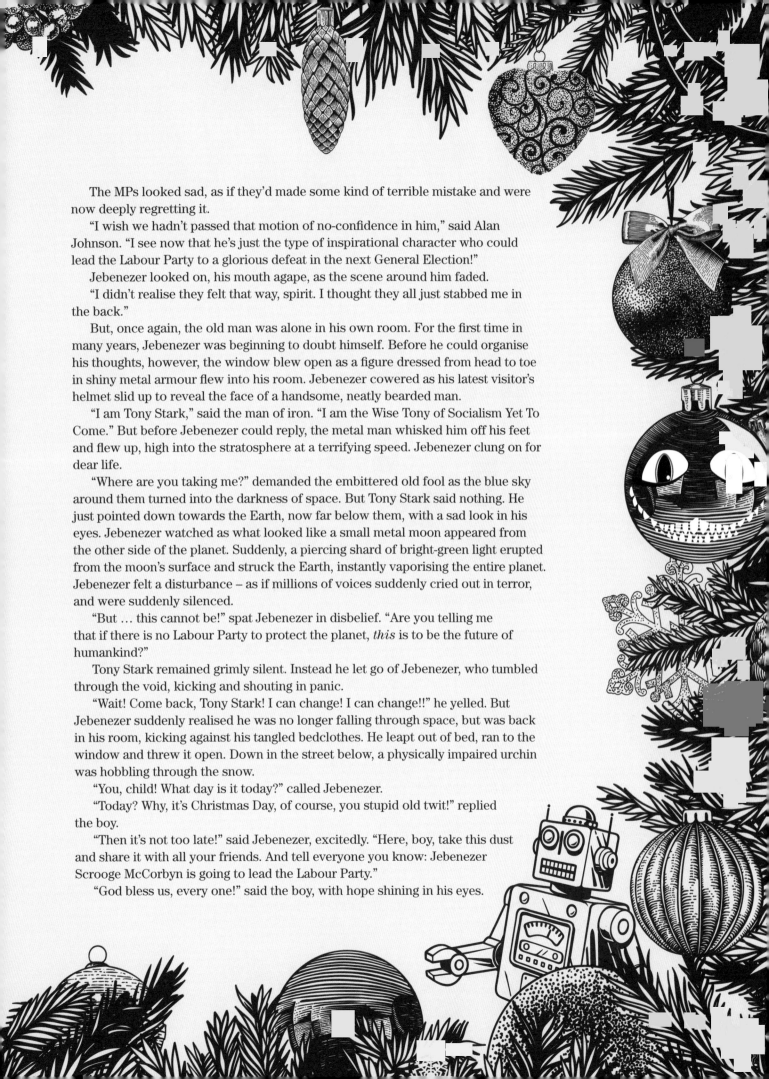

Answers!

Corbyn Crossword

Jeremy Is The Word (Search)

Answers!

Jeremy's Lost the Plot Maze

Answer. *The last route is the correct route back to the compost heap avoiding all the corporate fat cats*

Corbyn's Brain Drain Game

Answer. *It's a trick - all toilets eventually lead to the sewers (drains)!*

Fun Colour-Me-In Dot-to-Dot Spot the Difference

In Jeremy's lunch box were:
1 *Bananas*
2 *Apple*
3 *Gooseberries*
4 *Gherkin*

Differences
1 *Banana - 115 has been swapped with 116*
2 *Apple - 93 has been swapped with 94*
3 *Gooseberries - A tricky one this - both 16 & 17, and 34 & 35 have been swapped around*
4 *Gherkin – 68 has been swapped with 69*

Photo Credits

Alamy.com: page 7, Jason Bye / Alamy Stock Photo; page 15, Nathan King / Alamy Stock Photo; page 17 (top right), Mark Kerrison / Alamy Stock Photo; page 17 (bottom right), WENN Ltd / Alamy Stock Photo; page 18, Robert Melen / Alamy Stock Photo; page 24, Russell Hart / Alamy Stock Photo; page 27, Allstar Picture Library / Alamy Stock Photo; page 28, Allstar Picture Library / Alamy Stock Photo; page 29, David Mansell / Alamy Stock Photo; page 30, Prixpics / Alamy Stock Photo; page 35, Finnbarr Webster Editorial / Alamy Stock Photo; page 38, Jada Images / Alamy Stock Photo; page 39, Jason Bye / Alamy Stock Photo; page 70 (left), WENN Ltd / Alamy Stock Photo; page 70 (right), WENN Ltd / Alamy Stock Photo; page 71 (right), WENN Ltd / Alamy Stock Photo; page 71(bottom), Jack Taylor / Alamy Stock Photo.

Shutterstock.com: page14, Twocoms / Shutterstock.com; page 16 (bottom left), Victoria M Gardner / shutterstock.com; page34, Twocoms / Shutterstock.com; pages 40-41, Twocoms / shutterstock.com; page 42, Twocoms / Shutterstock.com; page 43, Ms Jane Campbell / Shutterstock.com; page 44, Twocoms / Shutterstock.com; pages 45 & 58, Twocoms / Shutterstock.com; page 54, 360b / Shutterstock.com; page 62, Frederic Legrand - COMEO / Shutterstock.com; page 71 (top left), Debby Wong / Shutterstock.com; page 74, Twocoms / Shutterstock.com

Acknowledgements

Photostory courtesy of My Guy magazine/Best of My Guy PhotoStories (Pavilion Books).

Comic strips illustrated by Becky Brice.

Thanks to Ellie Wyatt and Chris Harvey.

And thanks to Caron McQueen for the initial idea and all the other stuff.